Impressum
Verlag: BABADADA GmbH, Nedderfeld 112 , 22529 Hamburg
Geschäftsführer / Verlagsleitung: Harald Hof
Druck: Books on Demand GmbH, In de Tarpen 42, 22848 Norderstedt

Imprint
Publisher: BABADADA GmbH, Nedderfeld 112 , 22529 Hamburg, Germany
Managing Director / Publishing direction: Harald Hof
Print: Books on Demand GmbH, In de Tarpen 42, 22848 Norderstedt

school
škola

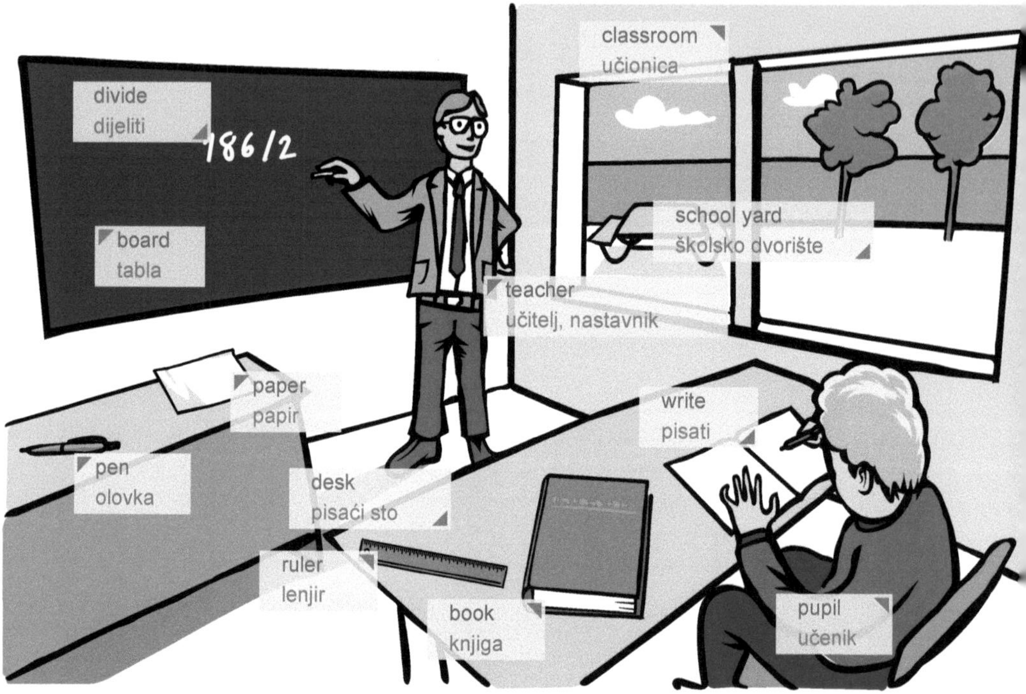

divide
dijeliti
186/2
board
tabla
classroom
učionica
school yard
školsko dvorište
teacher
učitelj, nastavnik
paper
papir
write
pisati
pen
olovka
desk
pisaći sto
ruler
lenjir
book
knjiga
pupil
učenik

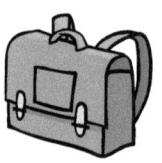

satchel
torba

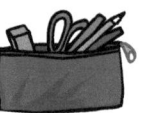

pencil case
pernica

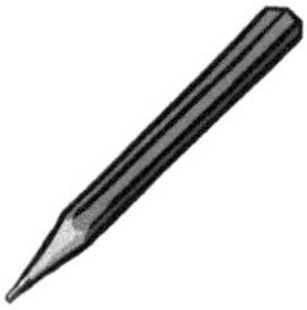

pencil
drvena olovka

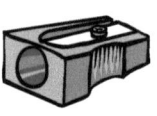

pencil sharpener
šiljalo za olovke

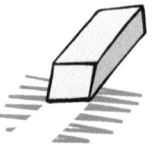

rubber
gumica

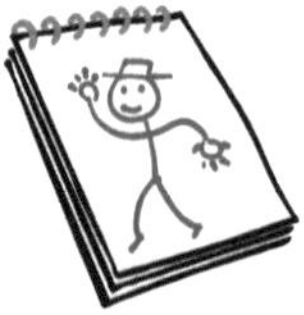

drawing pad
blok za crtanje

drawing

crtež

paintbrush

kist

paint box

kutija s bojama

scissors

makaze

glue

ljepilo

exercise book

vježbanka

homework

domaća zadaća

number

broj

add

sabirati

subtract

oduzimati

multiply

množiti

calculate

računati

letter

slovo

alphabet

abeceda

word

riječ

text
tekst

read
čitati

chalk
kreda

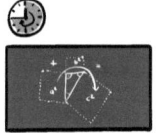

lesson
sat

register
školski dnevnik

examination
ispit

certificate
svjedočanstvo

school uniform
školska uniforma

education
izobrazba

encyclopedia
leksikon

university
univerzitet

microscope
mikroskop

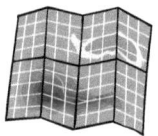

map
karta

waste-paper basket
korpa za papir

travel
putovanje

hotel
hotel
Grand
hostel
hostel
ROOMS
EXCHANGE
currency exchange office
mjenjačnica
car
auto

language

jezik

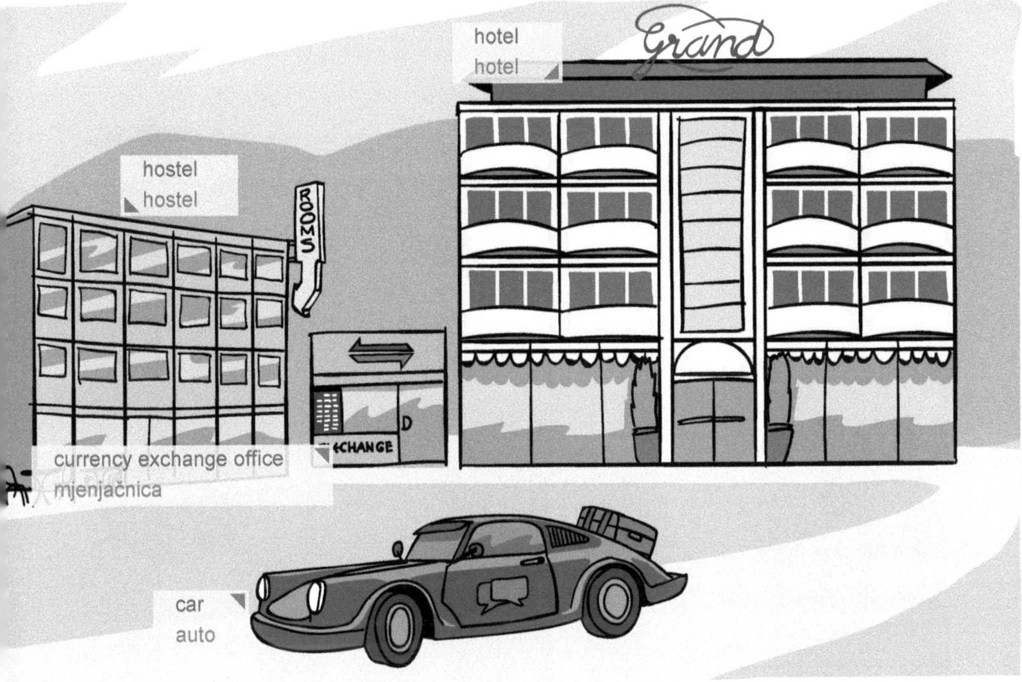

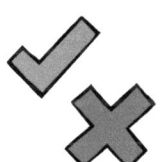

yes / no

da / ne

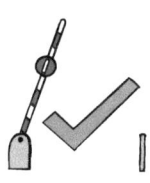

Okay

okej

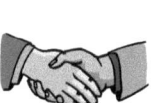

hello

zdravo

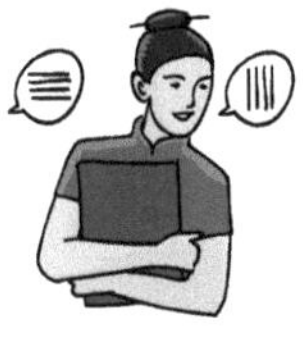

translator

tumač

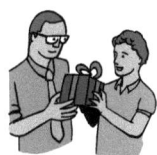

Thank you

hvala

how much is...?

Koliko košta...?

I don´t get it

Ne razumijem

problem

problem

Good evening!

dobro veče!

Good morning!

Dobro jutro!

Good night!

Laku noć!

goodbye

doviđenja

direction

smjer

luggage

prtljag

bag

torba

backpack

ruksak

guest

gost

room

soba

sleeping bag

vreća za spavanje

tent

šator

travel - putovanje

tourist information

turističke informacije

beach

plaža

credit card

kreditna kartica

breakfast

doručak

lunch

ručak

dinner

večera

Ticket

putna karta

elevator

lift

stamp

poštanska markica

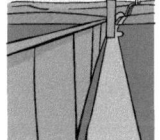

border

granica

customs

carina

embassy

ambasada

visa

viza

passport

pasoš

transport
transport

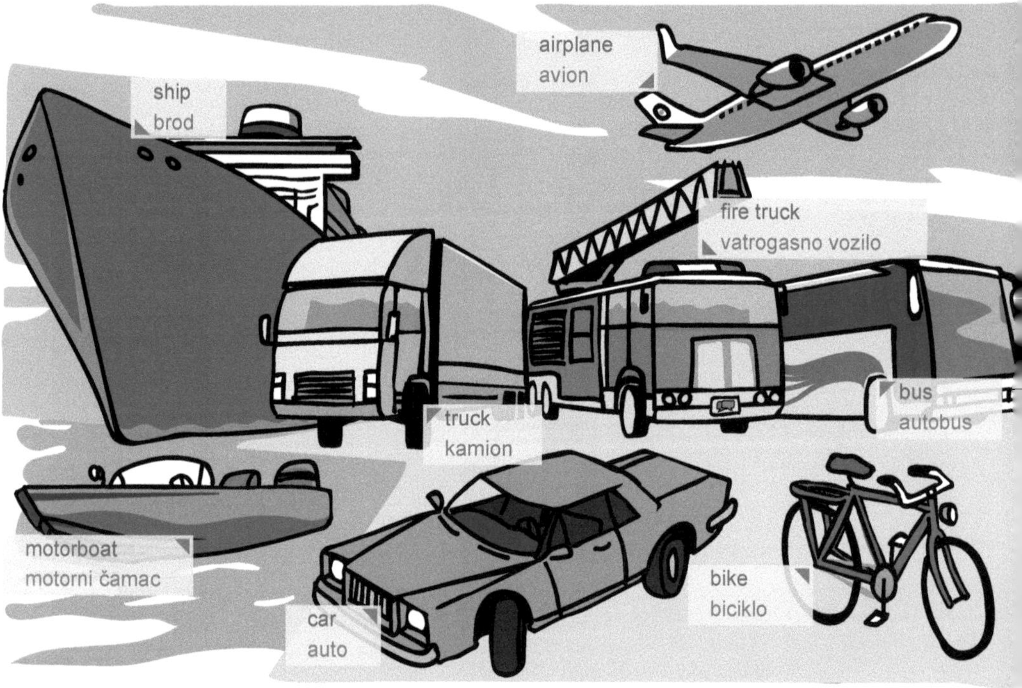

airplane
avion
ship
brod
fire truck
vatrogasno vozilo
bus
autobus
truck
kamion
motorboat
motorni čamac
bike
biciklo
car
auto

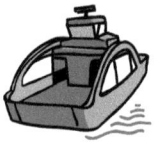

ferry
trajekt

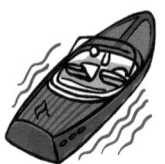

boat
brod

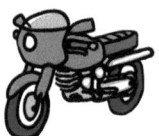

motorbike
motocikl

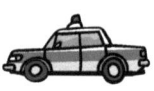

police car
policijski automobil

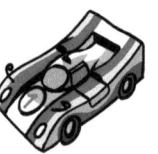

racing car
trkaći automobil

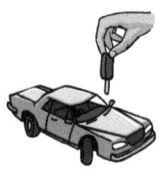

rental car
unajmljeni automobil

car sharing

kar-šering

tow truck

pauk

garbage truck

smećarsko vozilo

engine

motor

fuel

gorivo

fuel station

benzinska pumpa

traffic sign

saobraćajni znak

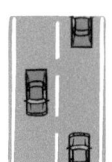

traffic

saobraćaj

traffic jam

zastoj

parking lot

parking

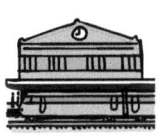

train station

željeznička stanica

tracks

šine

train

voz

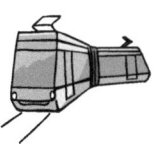

tram

tramvaj

wagon

vagon

transport - transport

helicopter

helikopter

airport

aerodrom

tower

toranj

passenger

putnik

container

kontejner

carton

karton

cart

tačke

basket

korpa

take off / land

poletjeti / sletjeti

city

grad

village

selo

city center

centar grada

house

kuća

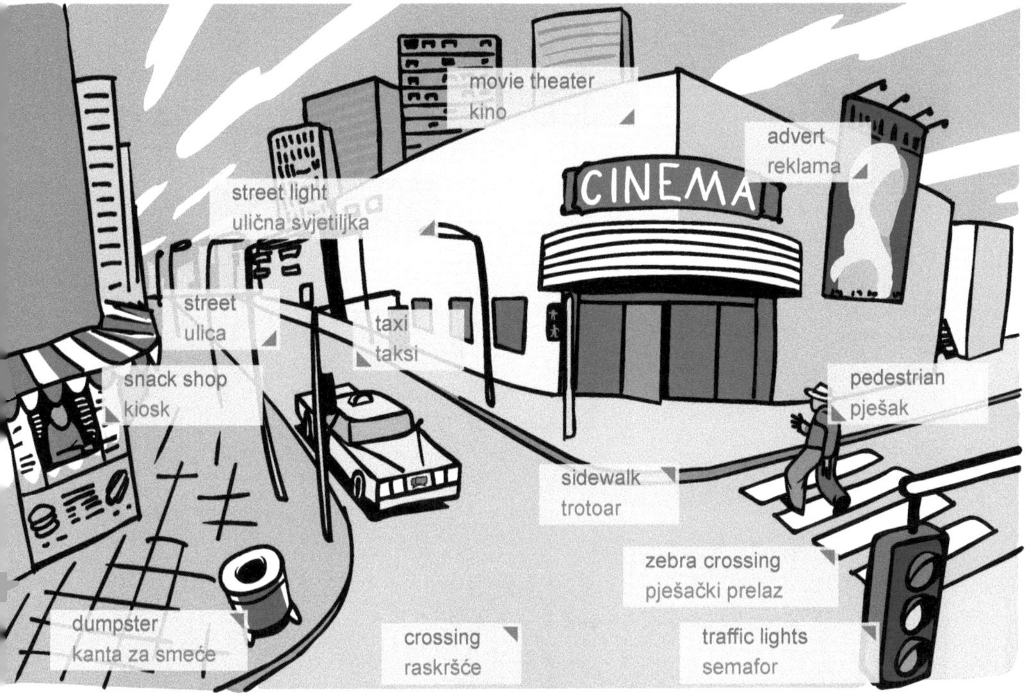

movie theater
kino

advert
reklama

street light
ulična svjetiljka

CINEMA

street
ulica

taxi
taksi

pedestrian
pješak

snack shop
kiosk

sidewalk
trotoar

zebra crossing
pješački prelaz

dumpster
kanta za smeće

crossing
raskršće

traffic lights
semafor

hut

koliba

apartment

stan

train station

željeznička stanica

city hall

vjećnica

museum

muzej

school

škola

university

univerzitet

bank

banka

hospital

bolnica

hotel

hotel

pharmacy

apoteka

office

ured

book shop

knjižara

shop

radnja

flower shop

cvjećara

supermarket

supermarket

market

pijaca

department store

robna kuća

fishmonger's shop

prodavač ribe

mall

trgovački centar

harbor

luka

park

park

bench

klupa

bridge

most

stairs

stepenice

subway

podzemna željeznica

tunnel

tunel

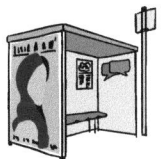

bus stop

autobuska stanica

bar

bar

restaurant

restoran

postbox

poštanski sandučić

street sign

saobraćajni znak

parking meter

sat za naplatu parkinga

zoo

zoološki vrt

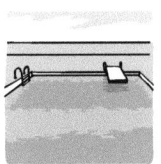

swimming pool

bazen

mosque

džamija

farm
seosko imanje

pollution
zagađenje okoline

cemetery
groblje

church
crkva

playground
igralište

temple
hram

landscape
krajolik

signpost
putokaz

path
putokaz

meadow
livada

stone
kamen

hiker
putnik

tree
drvo

river
rijeka

grass
trava

flower
cvijet

valley

dolina

hill

brdo

lake

jezero

forest

šuma

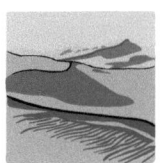

desert

pustinja

volcano

vulkan

castle

dvorac

rainbow

duga

mushroom

gljiva

palm tree

palma

mosquito

komarac

fly

muha

ant

mrav

bee

pčela

spider

pauk

landscape - krajolik

15

beetle

buba

frog

žaba

squirrel

vjeverica

hedgehog

jež

hare

zec

owl

sova

bird

ptica

swan

labud

boar

divlja svinja

deer

jelen

moose

los

dam

brana

wind turbine

vjetrenjača

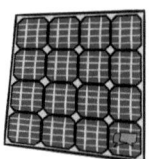

solar panel

solarni modul

climate

klima

restaurant
restoran

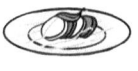

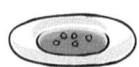

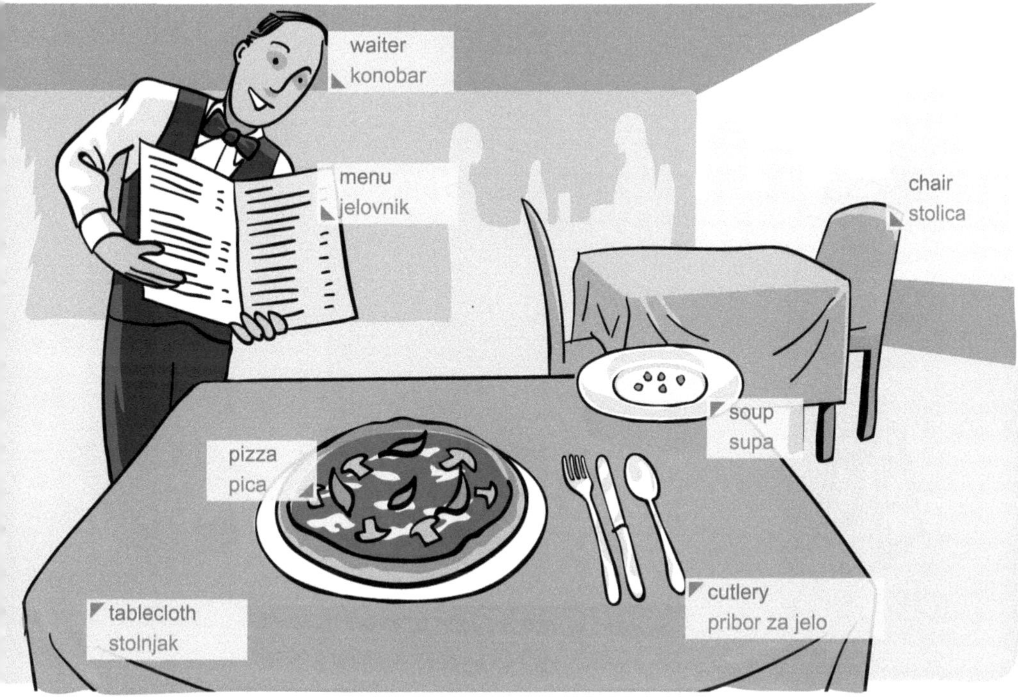

waiter
konobar
menu
jelovnik
chair
stolica
soup
supa
pizza
pica
tablecloth
stolnjak
cutlery
pribor za jelo

starter
predjelo

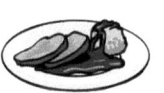

main course
glavno jelo

dessert
desert

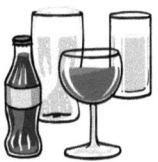

drinks
piće

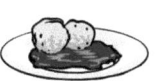

food
jelo

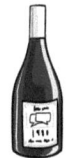

bottle
flaša

fast food
brza hrana

street food
jelo sa ulice

teapot
čajnik

sugar bowl
šećernica

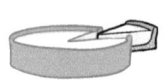

portion
porcija

espresso machine
mašina za espreso

high chair
barska stolica

bill
račun

tray
tacna

knife
nož

fork
viljuška

spoon
kašika

teaspoon
kašičica

serviette
salveta

glass
čaša

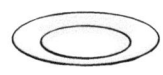

plate
tanjir

soup plate
tanjir za supu

saucer
tanjurić

sauce
sos

salt shaker
solanik

pepper mill
mlin za biber

vinegar
sirće

oil
ulje

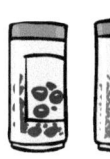

spices
začini

ketchup
kečap

mustard
senf

mayonnaise
majoneza

supermarket
supermarket

special offer
ponuda
FOR
customer
klijent
dairy products
mliječni proizvodi
fruit
voće
shopping cart
kolica za kupovinu

BUTCHERS

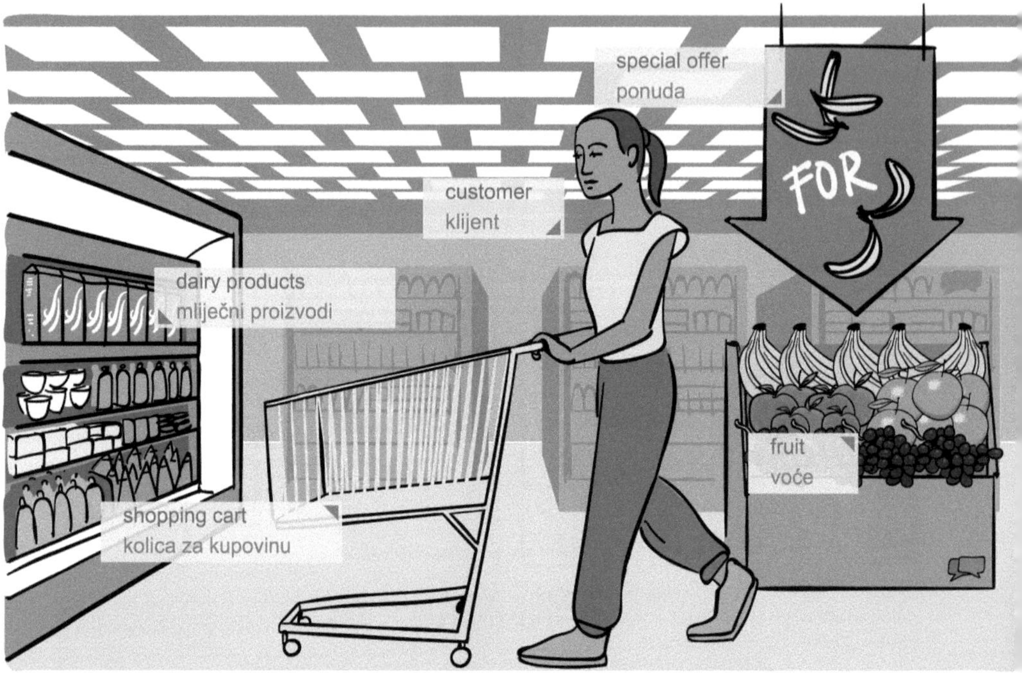

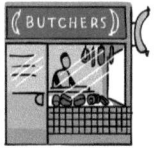

butcher's shop
mesnica- klaonica

BAKERY

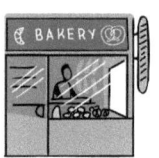

bakery
pekara

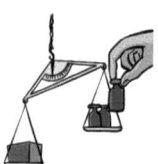

weigh
vagati

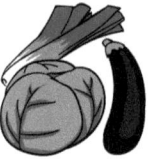

vegetables
povrće

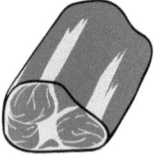

meat
meso

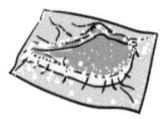

frozen food
zaleđena hrana

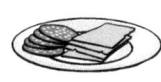

cold cuts
narezak

canned food
konzerve

detergent
prašak za veš

candy
slatkiši

household products
kućanski proizvodi

cleaning products
sredstvo za čišćenje

sales representative
prodavačica

cash register
kasa

cashier
blagajnik

shopping list
lista za kupovinu

opening hours
radno vrijeme

wallet
novčanik

credit card
kreditna kartica

bag
torba

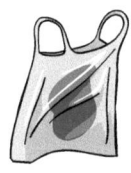

plastic bag
najlonska vrećica

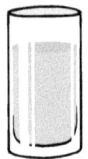

water
voda

juice
sok

milk
mlijeko

coke
kola

wine
vino

beer
pivo

alcohol
alkohol

cocoa
kakao

tea
čaj

coffee
kafa

espresso
espreso

cappuccino
kapućino

banana

banana

apple

jabuka

orange

narandža

melon

lubenica

lemon

limun

carrot

mrkva

garlic

bijeli luk

bamboo

bambus

onion

crveni luk

mushroom

gljiva

nuts

orašasti plodovi

noodles

pasta

spaghetti

špagete

rice

riža

salad

salata

fries

pomfrit

fried potatoes

pečeni krompir

pizza

pica

hamburger

hamburger

sandwich

sendvič

escalope

šnicla

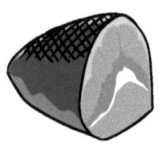

ham

šunka

salami

kobasica

sausage

kobasica

chicken

kokoš

roast

pečenje

fish

riba

porridge oats

zobene pahuljice

muesli

muzli

cornflakes

kornfleks

flour

brašno

croissant

kroason

bread roll

zemičke

bread

kruh

toast

tost

cookies

keksi

butter

maslac

curd

svježi sir

cake

kolač

egg

jaje

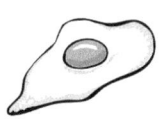

fried egg

jaje na oko

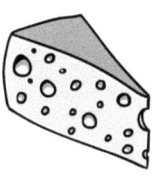

cheese

sir

ice cream

sladoled

sugar

šećer

honey

med

jelly

marmelada

nougat cream

nugat krema

curry

kuri

farm

seosko imanje

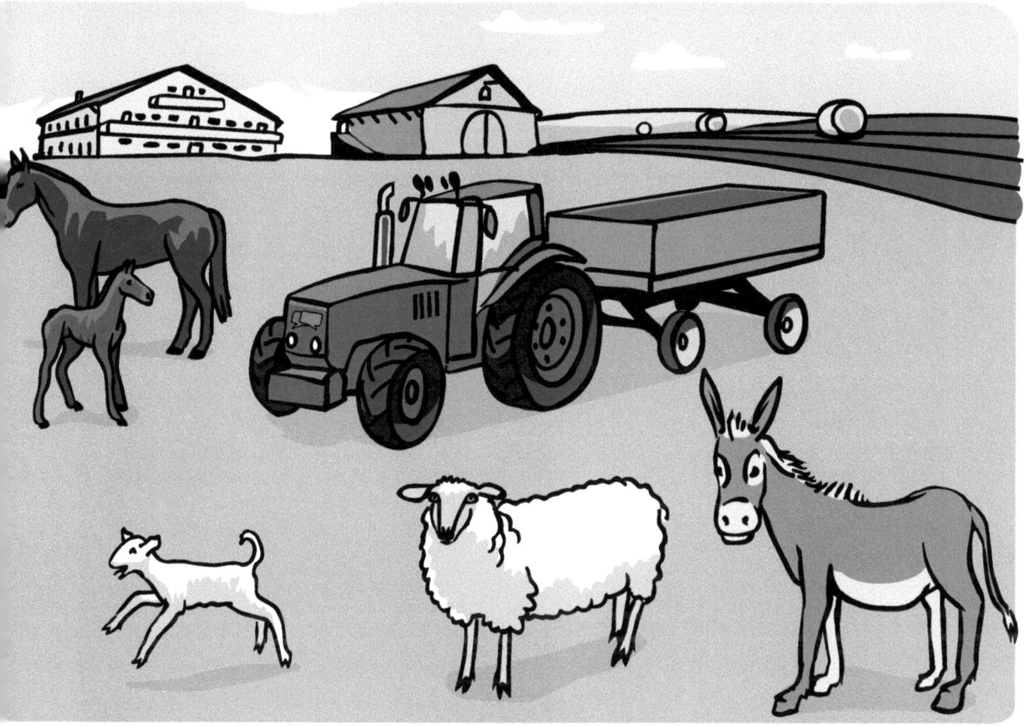

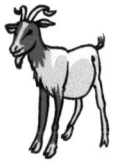

goat

koza

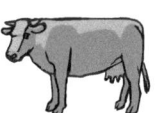

cow

krava

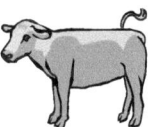

calf

tele

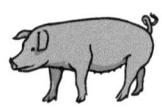

pig

svinja

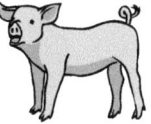

piglet

prase

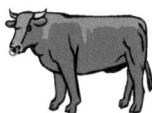

bull

bik

goose

guska

duck

patka

chick

pile

hen

kokoška

cockerel

pjetao

rat

pacov

cat

mačka

mouse

miš

ox

vol

dog

pas

dog house

pseća kućica

garden hose

crijevo za baštu

watering can

kanta za zalijevanje

scythe

kosa

plow

plug

sickle

srp

hoe

motika

pitchfork

vile

axe

sjekira

pushcart

tačke

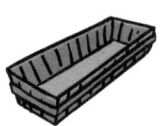

trough

korito

milk can

bokal za mlijeko

sack

vreća

fence

ograda

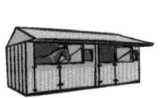

stable

štala

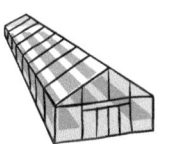

greenhouse

staklenik

soil

tlo

seed

sjeme

fertilizer

đubrivo

combine harvester

kombajn

farm - seosko imanje

harvest

kositi

harvest

žetva

yams

jam korijen

wheat

pšenica

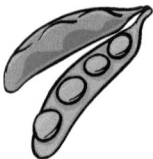

soya

soja

potato

krompir

corn

kukuruz

rapeseed

uljana repica

fruit tree

drvo voća

manioc

manioka

grain

žito

house
kuća

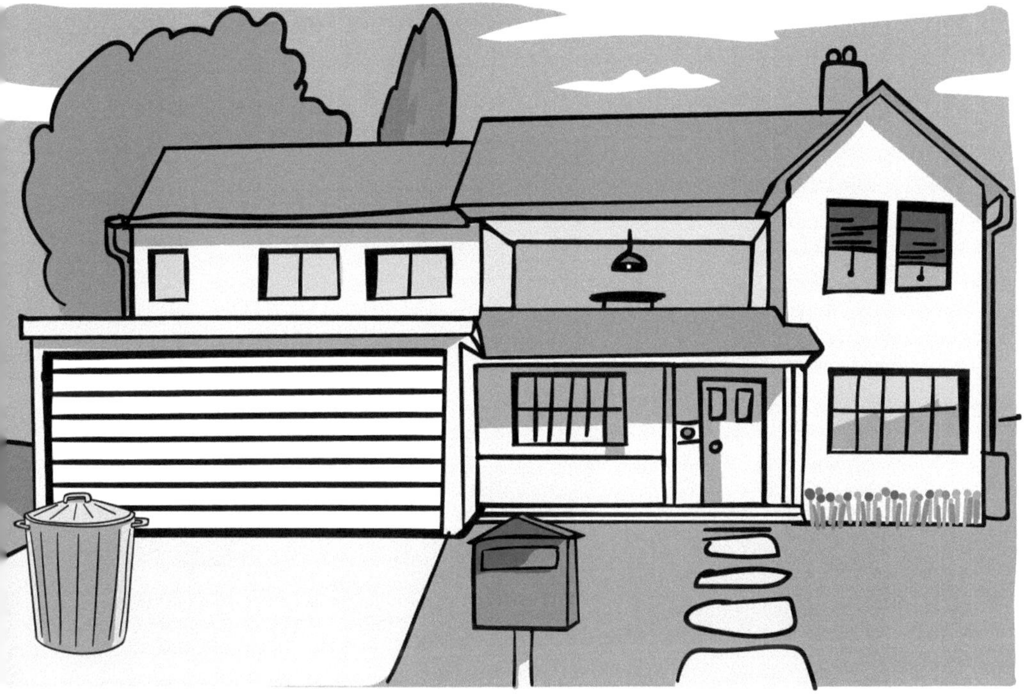

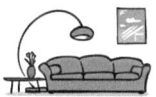

living room
....
dnevni boravak

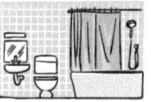

bathroom
....
kupatilo

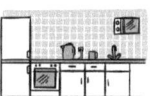

kitchen
....
kuhinja

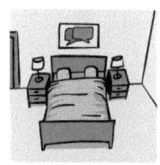

bedroom
....
spavaća soba

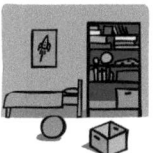

kids room
....
dječija soba

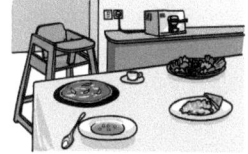

dining room
....
trpezarija

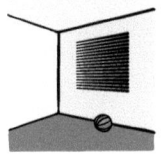

floor

pod, tlo

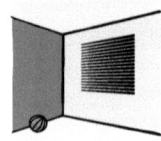

wall

zid

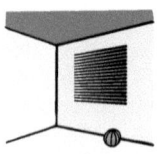

ceiling

plafon

cellar

podrum

sauna

sauna

balcony

balkon

terrace

terasa

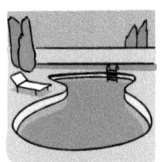

pool

bazen

lawn mower

kosilica

sheet

posteljina

bedspread

pokrivač

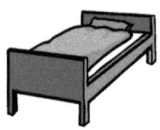

bed

krevet

broom

metla

bucket

kanta

switch

prekidač

living room
dnevni boravak

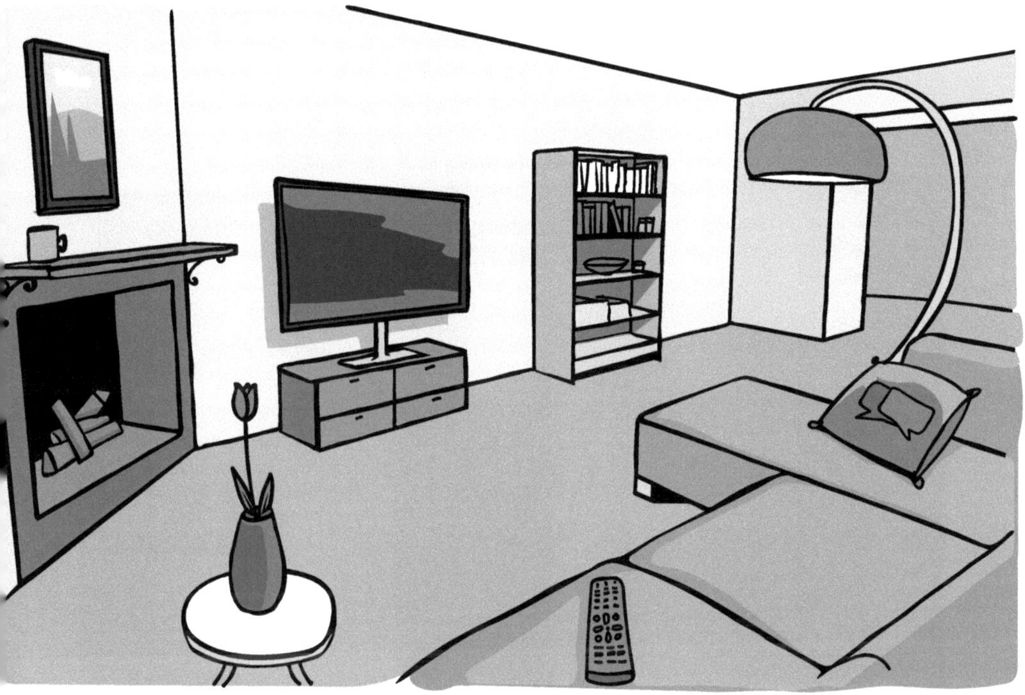

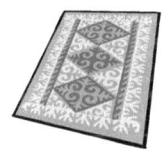

carpet

tepih

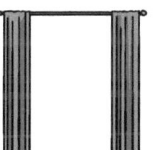

drape

zavjesa

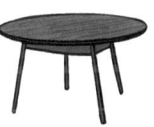

table

stol

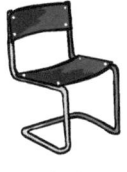

chair

stolica

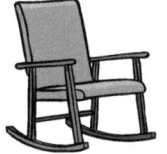

rocking chair

stolica za ljuljanje

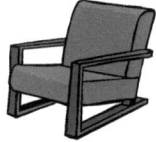

armchair

fotelja

book

knjiga

blanket

deka

decoration

dekoracija

firewood

ložno drvo

film

film

stereo system

stereo uređaj

key

ključ

newspaper

novine

painting

umjetnička slika

poster

poster

radio

radio

notebook

blok za bilješke

vacuum cleaner

usisavač

cactus

kaktus

candle

svijeća

kitchen
kuhinja

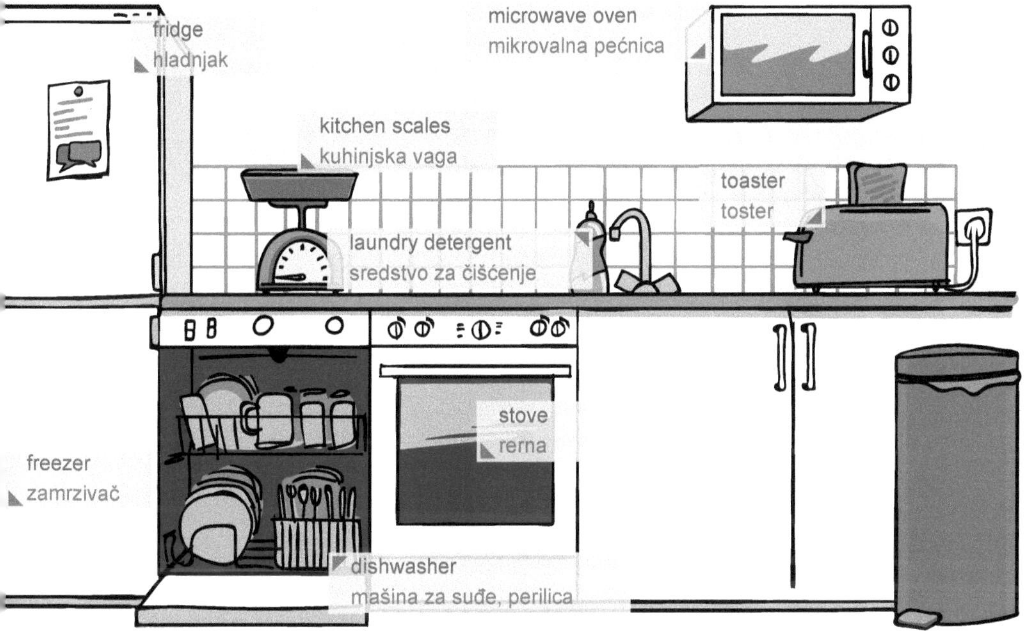

fridge
hladnjak
microwave oven
mikrovalna pećnica
kitchen scales
kuhinjska vaga
toaster
toster
laundry detergent
sredstvo za čišćenje
stove
rerna
freezer
zamrzivač
dishwasher
mašina za suđe, perilica

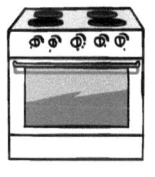

cooker

peć

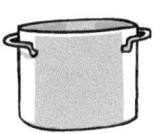

pot

lonac

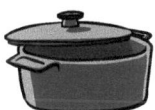

cast-iron pot

metalni lonac

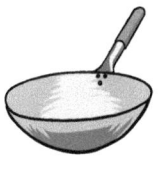

wok / kadai

vok / kadai

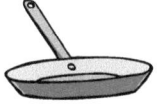

pan

tava, tiganj

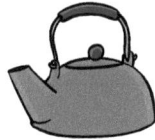

kettle

kuhalo

steamer

aparat za kuhanje na pari

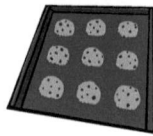

baking tray

lim za pečenje

crockery

posuđe

mug

šalica

bowl

činija

chopsticks

kineski štapići

ladle

kutlača

spatula

lopatica

whisk

metlica za snijeg bjelanjca

strainer

sito za kuhanje

sieve

sito

grater

ribež

mortar

avan s tučkom

barbecue

roštilj

fireplace

ložište

chopping board
daska

rolling pin
oklagija

corkscrew
vadičep

can
konzerva

can opener
otvarač za konzerve

oven cloth
krpe za lonac

sink
sudoper

brush
četka

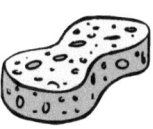

sponge
spužva

blender
mikser

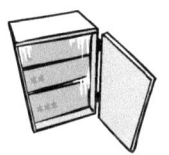

deep freezer
zamrzivač

baby bottle
flašica za bebu

tap
slavina

bathroom

kupatilo

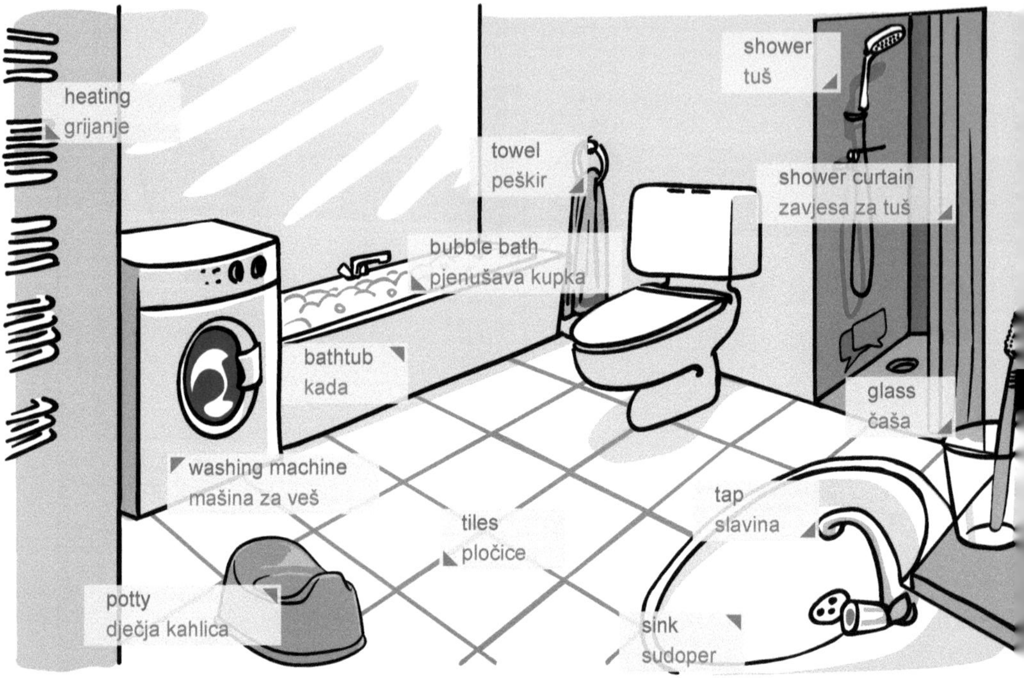

heating
grijanje
towel
peškir
shower
tuš
shower curtain
zavjesa za tuš
bubble bath
pjenušava kupka
bathtub
kada
glass
čaša
washing machine
mašina za veš
tap
slavina
tiles
pločice
potty
dječja kahlica
sink
sudoper

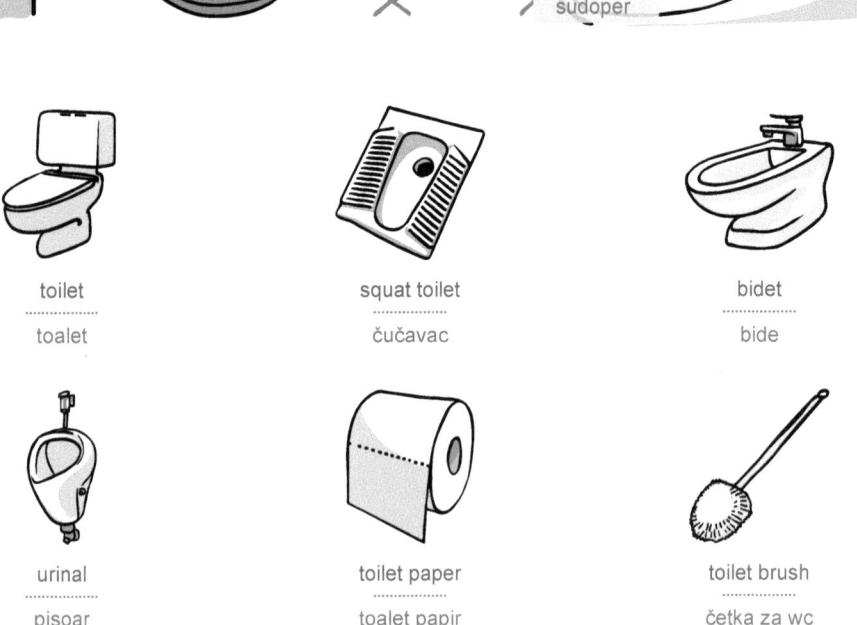

toilet

toalet

squat toilet

čučavac

bidet

bide

urinal

pisoar

toilet paper

toalet papir

toilet brush

četka za wc

toothbrush

četkica za zube

toothpaste

pasta za zube

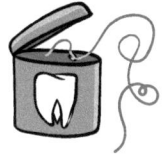

dental floss

zubni konac

wash

prati

hand shower

tuš

douche

intimni tuš

basin

lavor

back brush

četka za leđa

soap

sapun

shower gel

gel za tuširanje

shampoo

šampon

flannel

krpe za pranje

drain

odvod

creme

krema

deodorant

dezodorans

mirror

ogledalo

hand mirror

ogledalo za šminkanje

razor

brijač

shaving foam

pjena za brijanje

aftershave

vodica poslije brijanja

comb

češalj

brush

četka

hair-dryer

fen

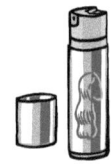

hairspray

sprej za kosu

makeup

puder

lipstick

karmin

nail varnish

lak za nokte

cotton wool

vata

nail scissors

makazice za nokte

perfume

parfem

washbag

kozmetička torbica

stool

hoklica

weighing scales

vaga

bathrobe

kupaći ogrtač

rubber gloves

rukavice za čišćenje

tampon

tampon

sanitary towel

uložak za dame

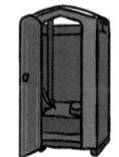

chemical toilet

hemijski toalet

kids room

dječija soba

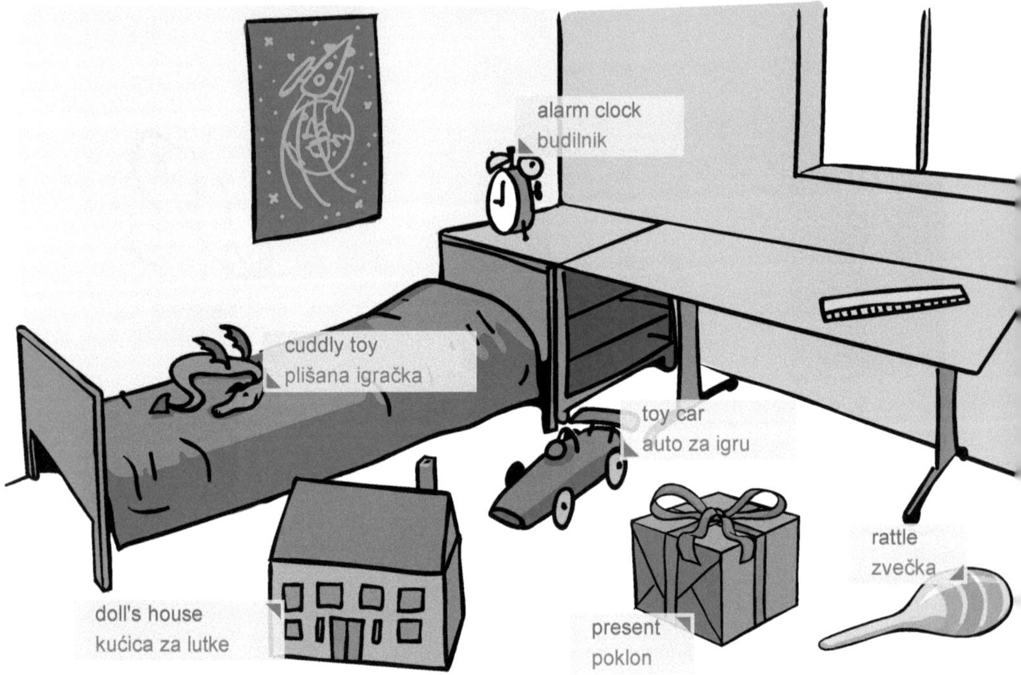

alarm clock
budilnik
cuddly toy
plišana igračka
toy car
auto za igru
rattle
zvečka
doll's house
kućica za lutke
present
poklon

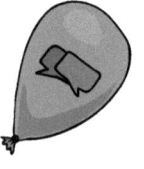

balloon

balon

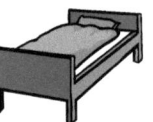

bed

krevet

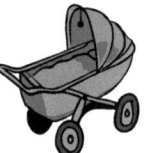

stroller

kolica za djecu

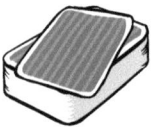

deck of cards

karte za igranje

jigsaw

puzle

SUPER MEGA

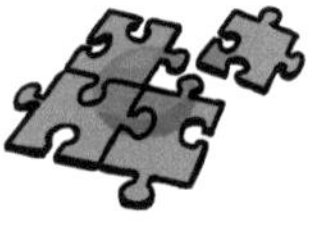

comic

strip

lego bricks

lego kockice

toy blocks

kockice za gradnju

action figure

akcione figure

romper suit

benkica

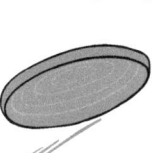

frisbee

frizbi

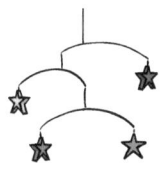

mobile

mobile

board game

igra na ploči

dice

kocka

model train set

miniatura željeznice

pacifier

cucla

party

zabava

picture book

slikovnica

ball

lopta

doll

lutka

play

igrati

sandpit

pješćanik

swing

ljuljačka

toys

igračke

video game console

konzola za igru

tricycle

triciklo

teddy bear

medvjedić

wardrobe

ormar

clothing

odjeća

socks

kratke čarape

stockings

čarape

tights

hulahopke

scarf
šal

umbrella
kišobran

t-shirt
majica kratkih rukava

belt
kaiš

boots
čizme

slippers
papuče

sneakers
patike

sandals
....
sandale

shoes
....
cipele

rubber boots
....
gumene čizme

underwear
....
gaće

bra
....
grudnjak

undershirt
....
potkošulja

clothing - odjeća

body

bodi

pants

hlače

jeans

farmerke

skirt

suknja

blouse

bluza

shirt

košulja

pullover

džemper

sweater

majica

blazer

sako

jacket

jakna

coat

mantil

raincoat

kišni mantil

costume

kostim

dress

haljina

wedding dress

vjenčanica

suit

odijelo

nightgown

spavaćica

pajamas

pidžama

sari

sari

headscarf

marama

turban

turban

burka

burka

kaftan

kaftan

abaya

abaja

swimsuit

kupaći kostim

trunks

kupaće gaće

shorts

kratke hlače

tracksuit

trenerka

apron

pregača

gloves

rukavice

button

dugme

glasses

naočare

bracelet

narukvica

necklace

ogrlica

ring

prsten

earring

naušnica

cap

kapa

coat hanger

vješalica

hat

šešir

tie

kravata

zip

patentni zatvarač

helmet

kaciga

braces

tregeri za hlače

school uniform

školska uniforma

uniform

uniforma

bib

podbradak

pacifier

cucla

diaper

pelene

office
ured

filing cabinet
ormar za kartoteku

server
server

paper
papir

printer
štampač

monitor
monitor

desk
pisaći sto

mouse
miš

folder
registrator

keyboard
tastatura

waste paper basket
korpa za papir

computer
kompjuter

chair
stolica

coffee mug

šolja za kafu

calculator

kalkulator

internet

internet

office - ured

laptop	letter	message
laptop	pismo	poruka

cell phone	network	photocopier
mobilni telefon	mreža	aparat za kopiranje

software	telephone	plug socket
softver	telefon	utičnica
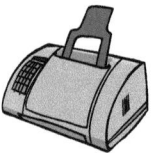	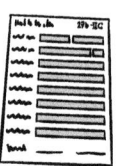	
fax machine	form	document
faks	formular	dokument

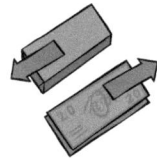

buy

kupovati

pay

platiti

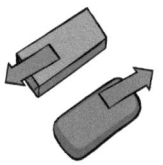

trade

trgovati

money

novac

 **USD**

dollar

dolar

EUR

euro

euro

 **JPY**

yen

jen

RUB

rouble

rublja

CHF

Swiss franc

franak

 **CNY**

renminbi yuan

renminbi jen

INR

rupee

rupi

cash point

bankomat

currency exchange office

mjenjačnica

gold

zlato

silver

srebro

oil

nafta

energy

energija

price

cijena

contract

ugovor

tax

porez

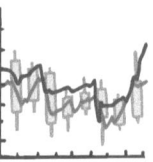

stock

akcija

work

raditi

employee

službenik

employer

poslodavac

factory

fabrika

shop

radnja

economy - ekonomija

occupations
zanimanja

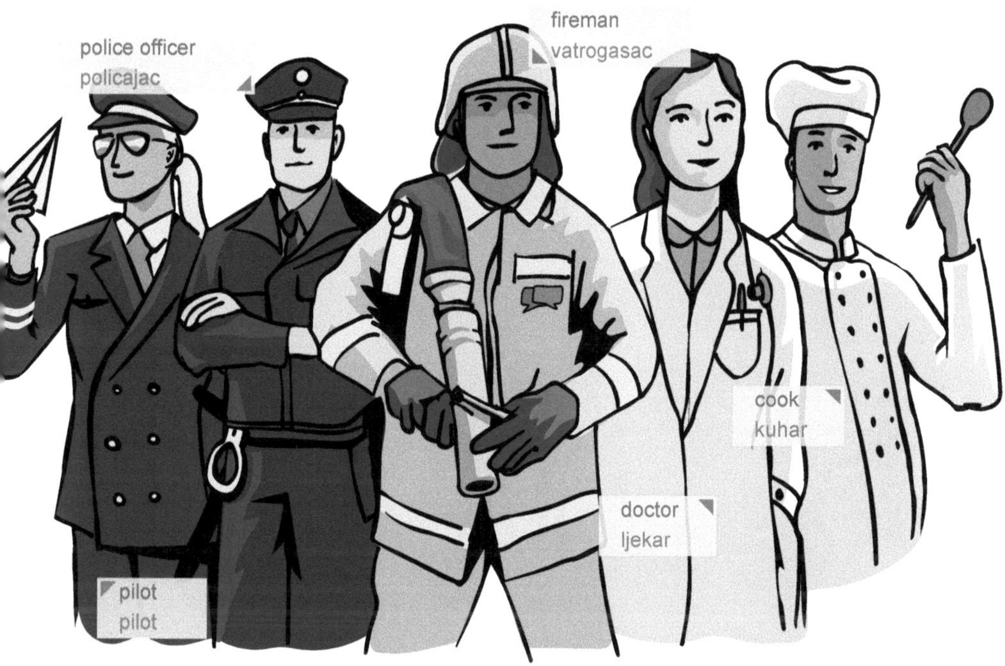

police officer
policajac
fireman
vatrogasac
cook
kuhar
doctor
ljekar
pilot
pilot

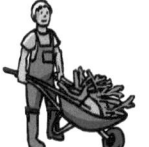

gardener
baštovan

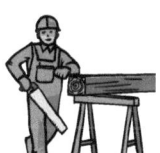

carpenter
stolar

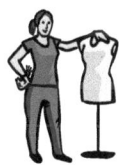

seamstress
krojačica

judge
sudija

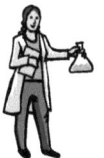

chemist
hemičar

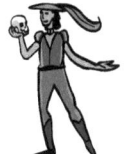

actor
glumac

bus driver	taxi driver	fisherman
vozač autobusa	vozač taksija	ribar

cleaning lady	roofer	waiter
čistačica	krovopokrivač	konobar

hunter	painter	baker
lovac	moler	pekar

electrician	builder	engineer
električar	građevinski radnik	inženjer

butcher	plumber	postman
koljač	limar, vodoinstalater	poštar

soldier

vojnik

architect

arhitekta

cashier

blagajnik

florist

cvjećar

hairdresser

frizer

conductor

kontrolor

mechanic

mehaničar

captain

kapiten

dentist

zubar

scientist

naučnik

rabbi

rabin

imam

imam

monk

monah

pastor

sveštenik

tools
alat

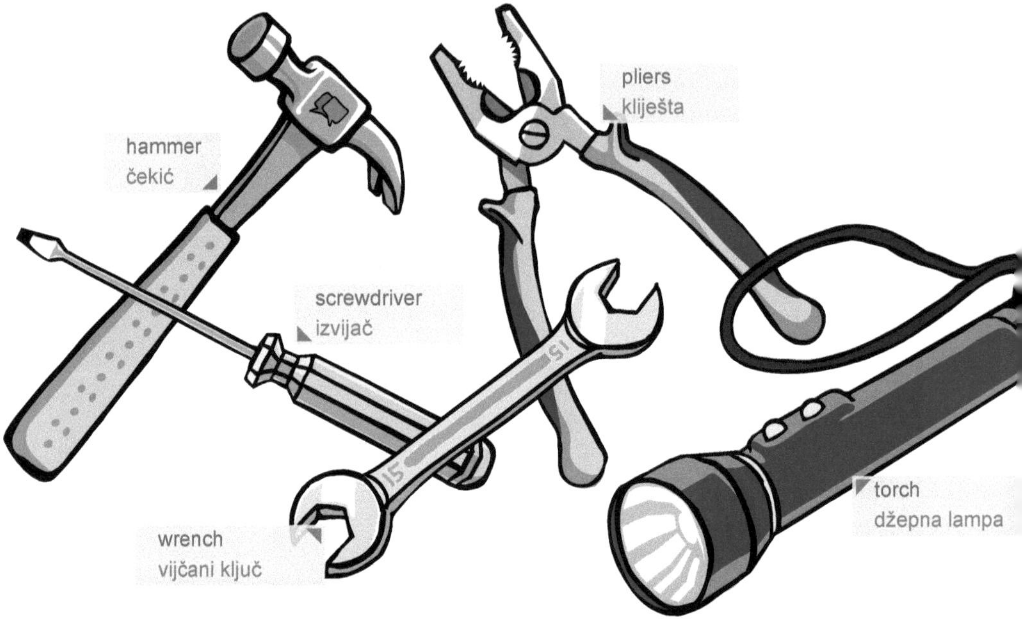

pliers
kliješta
hammer
čekić
screwdriver
izvijač
torch
džepna lampa
wrench
vijčani ključ

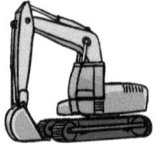

excavator
bager

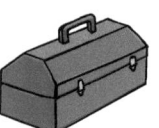

toolbox
kutija sa alatom

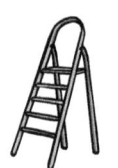

ladder
ljestve

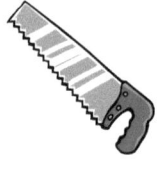

saw
testera, pila

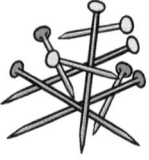

nails
ekser

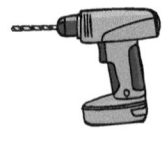

drill
bušilica

repair
popraviti

shovel
lopata

Damn!
sranje!

dustpan
lopatica

paint can
kanta boje

screws
vijak

musical instruments
muzički instrumenti

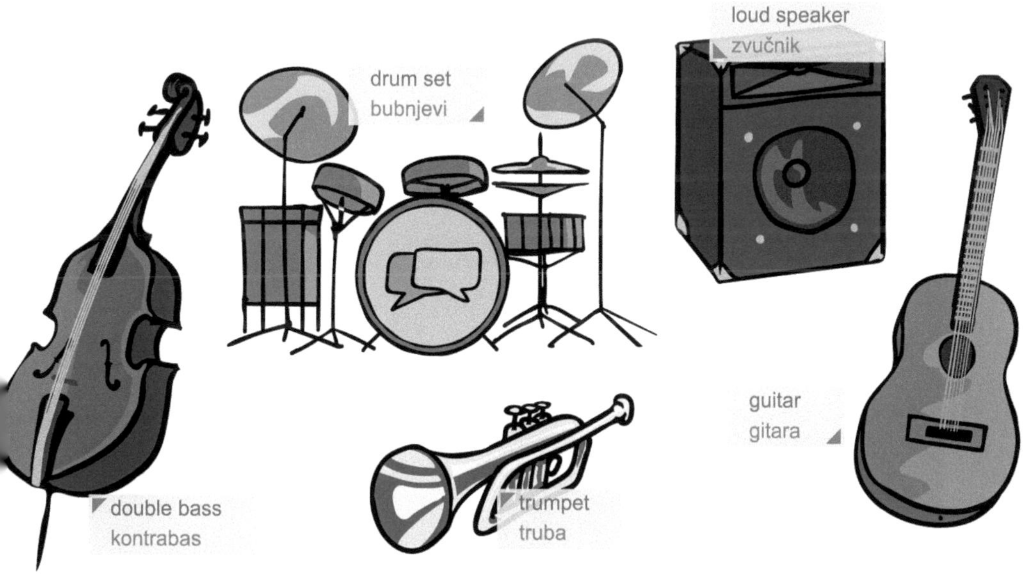

loud speaker
zvučnik

drum set
bubnjevi

guitar
gitara

double bass
kontrabas

trumpet
truba

piano

klavir

violin

violina

bass

bas

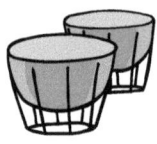

timpani

bubanj timpani

drums

bubanj

keyboard

sintisajzer

saxophone

saksofon

flute

flauta

microphone

mikrofon

zoo
zološki vrt

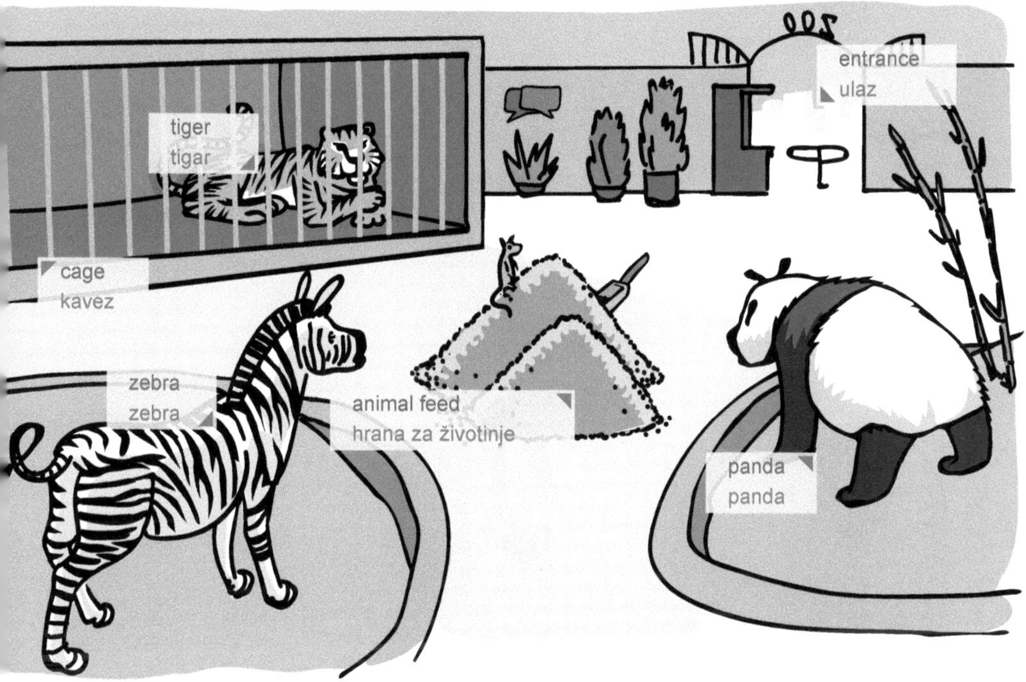

entrance
ulaz
tiger
tigar
cage
kavez
zebra
zebra
animal feed
hrana za životinje
panda
panda

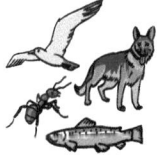

animals
životinje

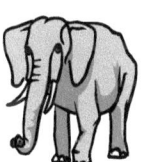

elephant
slon

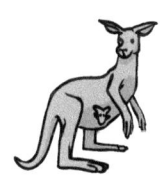

kangaroo
kengur

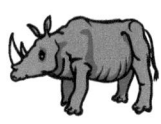

rhino
nosorog

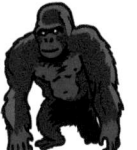

gorilla
gorila

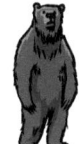

bear
medvjed

camel

kamila

ostrich

noj

lion

lav

monkey

majmun

flamingo

flamingo

parrot

papagaj

polar bear

polarni medvjed

penguin

pingvin

shark

morski pas

peacock

paun

snake

zmija

crocodile

krokodil

zookeeper

čuvar u zološkom vrtu

seal

tuljan

jaguar

jaguar

zoo - zoološki vrt

pony

poni

leopard

leopard

hippo

nilski konj

giraffe

žirafa

eagle

orao

boar

divlja svinja

fish

riba

turtle

kornjača

walrus

morž

fox

lisica

gazelle

gazela

American football
američki fudbal

cycling
vožnja bicikla

tennis
tenis

basketball
košarka

swimming
plivanje

boxing
boks

ice hockey
hokej na ledu

soccer
fudbal

badminton
bedminton

athletics
laka atletika

handball
rukomet

skiing
skijanje

polo
polo

activities
aktivnosti

jump
skakati
hug
zagrliti
laugh
smijati se
walk
ići
sing
pjevati
dream
sanjati
pray
moliti
kiss
ljubiti

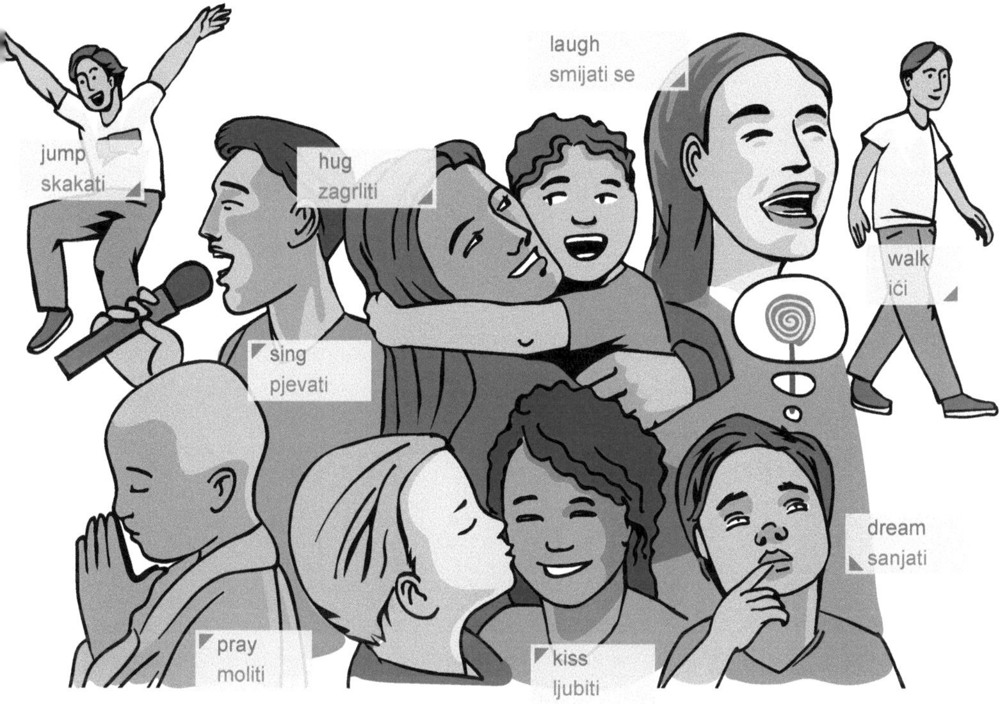

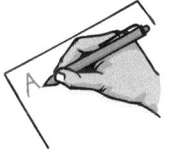

write
pisati

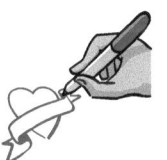

draw
crtati

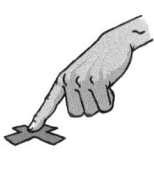

show
pokazati

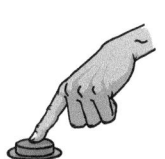

push
gurati

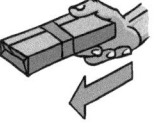

give
dati

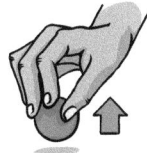

take
uzeti

have

imati

do

raditi

be

biti

stand

stajati

run

trčati

pull

vući

throw

baciti

fall

pasti

lie

ležati

wait

čekati

carry

nositi

sit

sjediti

get dressed

obući

sleep

spavati

wake up

probuditi

look at

pogledati

cry

plakati

stroke

milovati

comb

češljati

talk

govoriti

understand

razumjeti

ask

pitati

listen

slušati

drink

piti

eat

jesti

tidy up

pospremiti

love

voljeti

cook

kuhati

drive

voziti

fly

letjeti

activities - aktivnosti

sail

jedriti

calculate

računati

read

čitati

learn

učiti

work

raditi

marry

vjenčavti

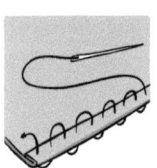

sew

šiti

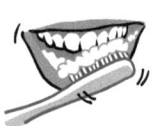

brush teeth

prati zube

kill

ubiti

smoke

pušiti

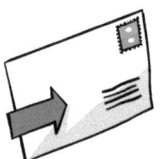

send

slati

family
porodica

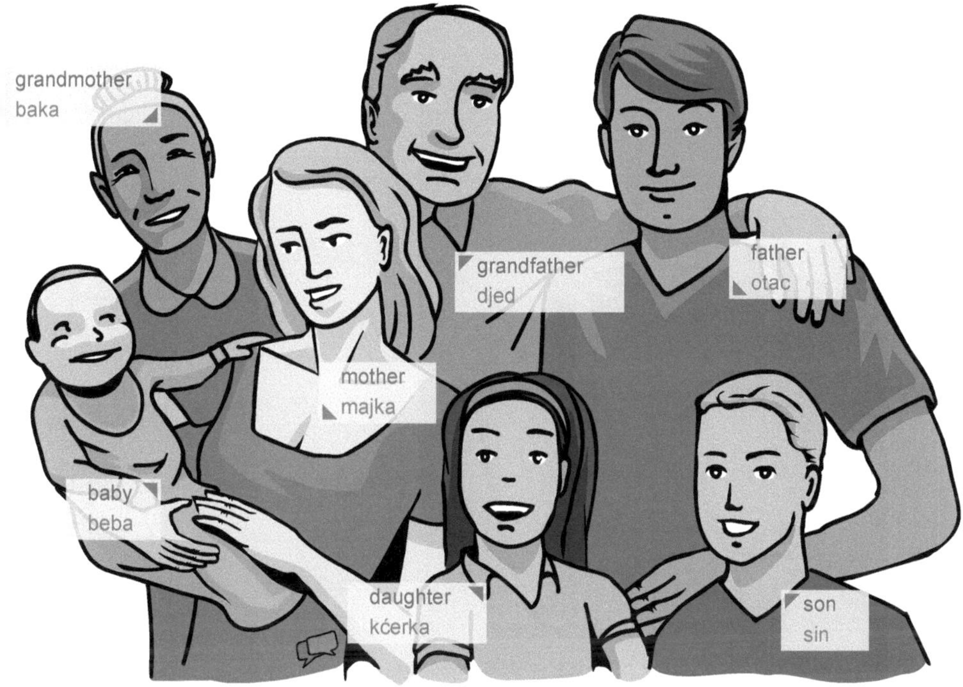
grandmother
baka
grandfather
djed
father
otac
mother
majka
baby
beba
daughter
kćerka
son
sin

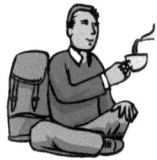

guest
gost

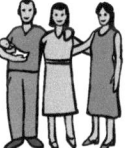

aunt
ujna, tetka, strina

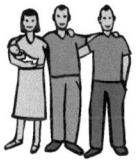

uncle
ujak, tetak, stric

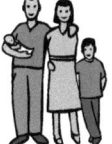

brother
brat

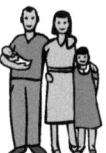

sister
sestra

body
tijelo

forehead
čelo
eye
oko
face
lice
chin
brada
breast
grudi
finger
prst
hand
ruka, šaka
arm
ruka
shoulder
leđa
leg
noga

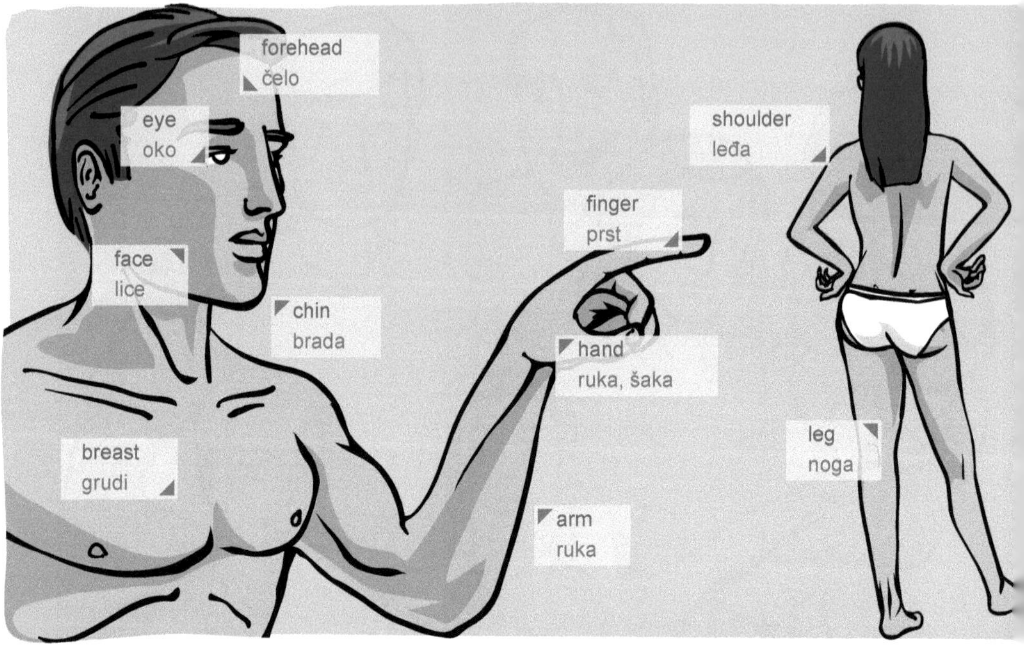

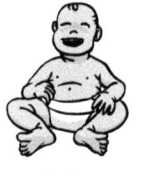

baby
beba

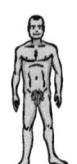

man
muškarac

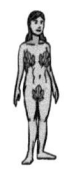

woman
žena

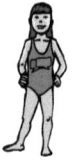

girl
djevojčica

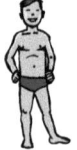

boy
dječak

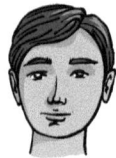

head
glava

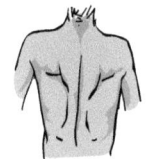

back

leđa

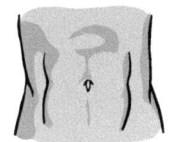

belly

stomak

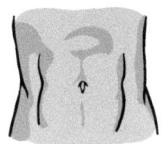

navel

pupak

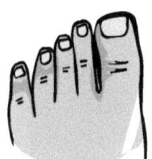

toe

nožni prst

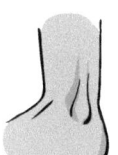

heel

peta

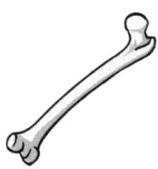

bone

kosti

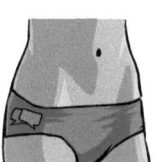

hip

kuk

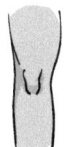

knee

koljeno

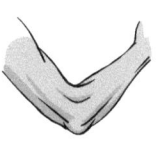

elbow

lakat

nose

nos

buttocks

stražnjica

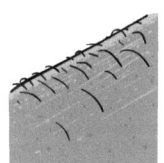

skin

koža

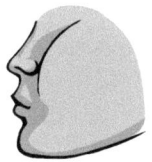

cheek

obraz

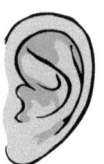

ear

uho

lip

usna

body - tijelo

mouth

usta

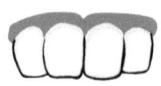

tooth

zub

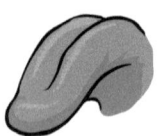

tongue

jezik

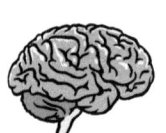

brain

mozak

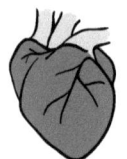

heart

srce

muscle

mišić

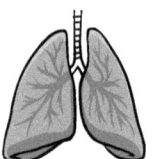

lung

pluća

liver

jetra

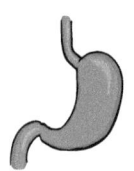

stomach

želudac

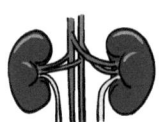

kidneys

bubreg

sex

spolni odnos

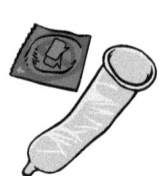

condom

kondom

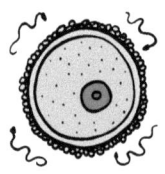

ovum

jajna ćelija

semen

sperma

pregnancy

trudnoća

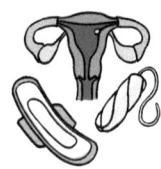

menstruation

menstruacija

vagina

vagina

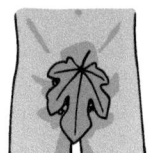

penis

penis

eyebrow

obrva

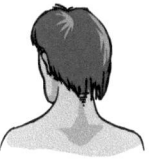

hair

kosa

neck

vrat

hospital
bolnica

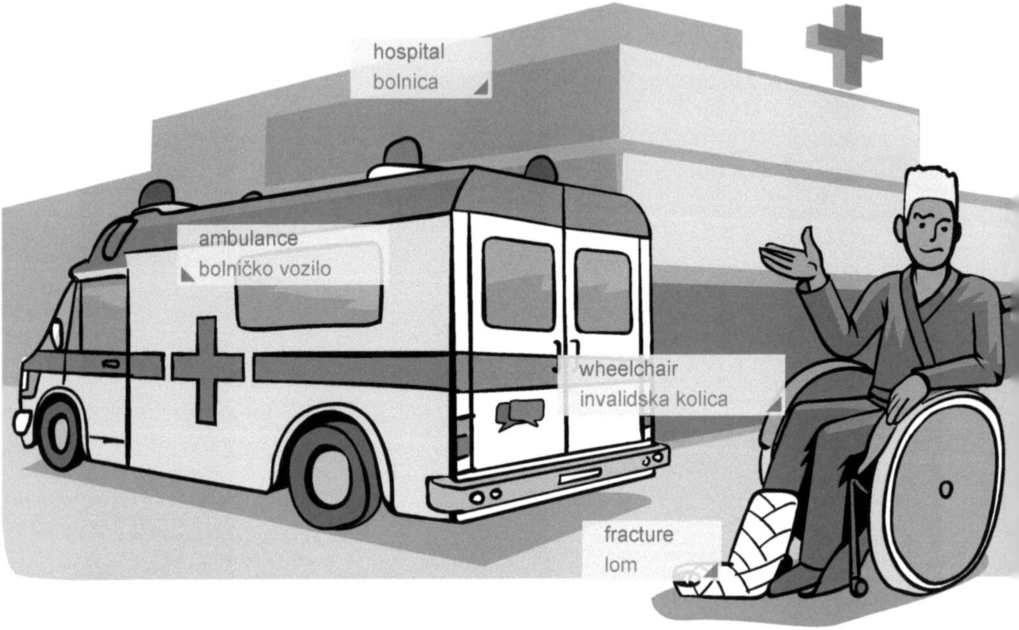

hospital
bolnica
ambulance
bolničko vozilo
wheelchair
invalidska kolica
fracture
lom

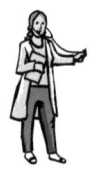

doctor

ljekar

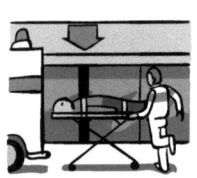

emergency room

hitna služba

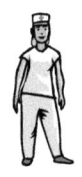

nurse

medicinska sestra

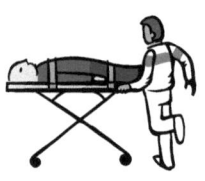

emergency

hitna pomoć

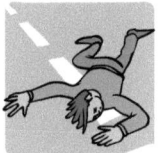

unconscious

nesvjest

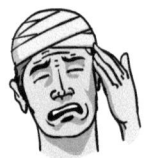

pain

bol

injury

povreda

bleeding

krvarenje

heart attack

srčani udar, infarkt

stroke

moždani udar

allergy

alergija

cough

kašalj

fever

groznica

flu

gripa

diarrhea

proljev

headache

glavobolja

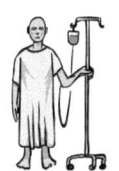

cancer

rak

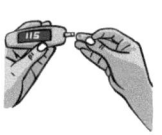

diabetes

dijabetes

surgeon

hirurg

scalpel

skalpel

operation

operacija

CT

CT

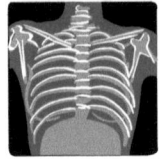

x-ray

rendgen

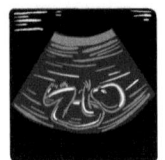

ultrasound

ultrazvuk

face mask

maska

disease

bolest

waiting room

čekaonica

crutch

štake

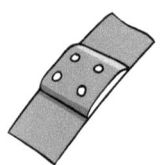

plaster

flaster

bandage

zavoj

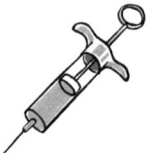

injection

injekcija

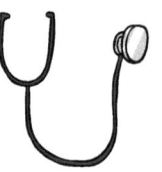

stethoscope

stetoskop

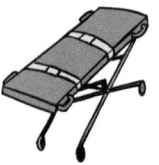

stretcher

nosilo

clinical thermometer

termometar

birth

porod

overweight

prekomjerna težina, debljina

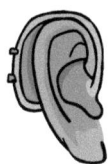

hearing aid
slušni aparat

disinfectant
sredstvo za dezinfekciju

infection
infekcija

virus
virus

HIV / AIDS
HIV/ AIDS

medicine
medicina

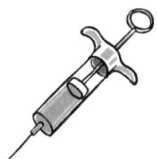

vaccination
vakcinacija

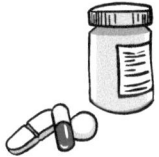

tablets
tablete

pill
pilula

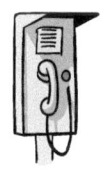

emergency call
hitni poziv

blood pressure monitor
aparat za mjerenje pritiska

ill / healthy
bolestan / zdrav

Help!	alarm	assault
Upomoć!	alarm	napad, prepad
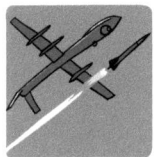		
attack	danger	emergency exit
napad	opasnost	izlaz u slučaju opasnosti

Fire!	fire extinguisher	accident
Požar!	vatrogasni aparat	nezgoda
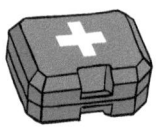		
first-aid kit	SOS	police
torba prve pomoći	SOS	policija

Europe

Europa

North America

Sjeverna Amerika

South America

Južna Amerika

Africa

Afrika

Asia

Azija

Australia

Australija

Atlantic

Atlantik

Pacific

Pacifik

Indian Ocean

Indijski okean

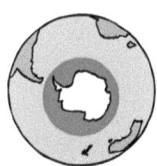

Antarctic Ocean

Antarktički okean

Arctic Ocean

Arktički okean

North pole

Sjeverni pol

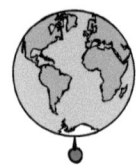

South pole

Južni pol

Antarctica

Antarktik

earth

Zemlja

land

zemlja

sea

more

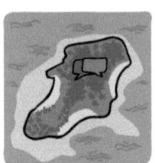

island

ostrvo

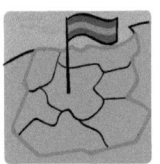

nation

nacija

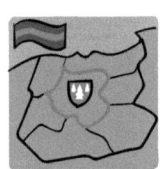

state

država

clock face

brojčanik sata

hour hand

kazaljka sata

minute hand

kazaljka minute

second hand

kazaljka sekunde

What time is it?

Koliko je sati?

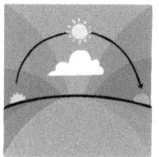

day

dan

time

vrijeme

now

sada

digital watch

digitalni sat

minute

minuta

hour

sat

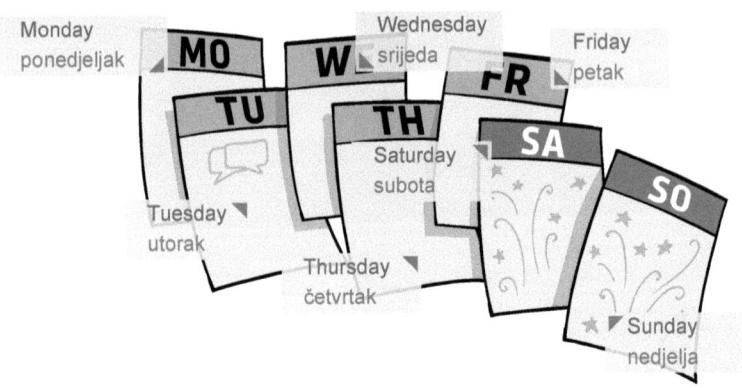

Monday — ponedjeljak
Wednesday — srijeda
Friday — petak
Saturday — subota
Tuesday — utorak
Thursday — četvrtak
Sunday — nedjelja

yesterday

juče

today

danas

tomorrow

sutra

morning

jutro

noon

podne

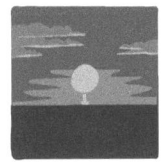

evening

veče

workdays

radni dani

weekend

vikend

year
godina

rain
kiša
wind
vjetar
snow
snijeg
spring
proljeće
summer
ljeto
fall
jesen
winter
zima

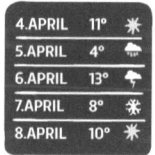

4.APRIL 11°
5.APRIL 4°
6.APRIL 13°
7.APRIL 8°
8.APRIL 10°

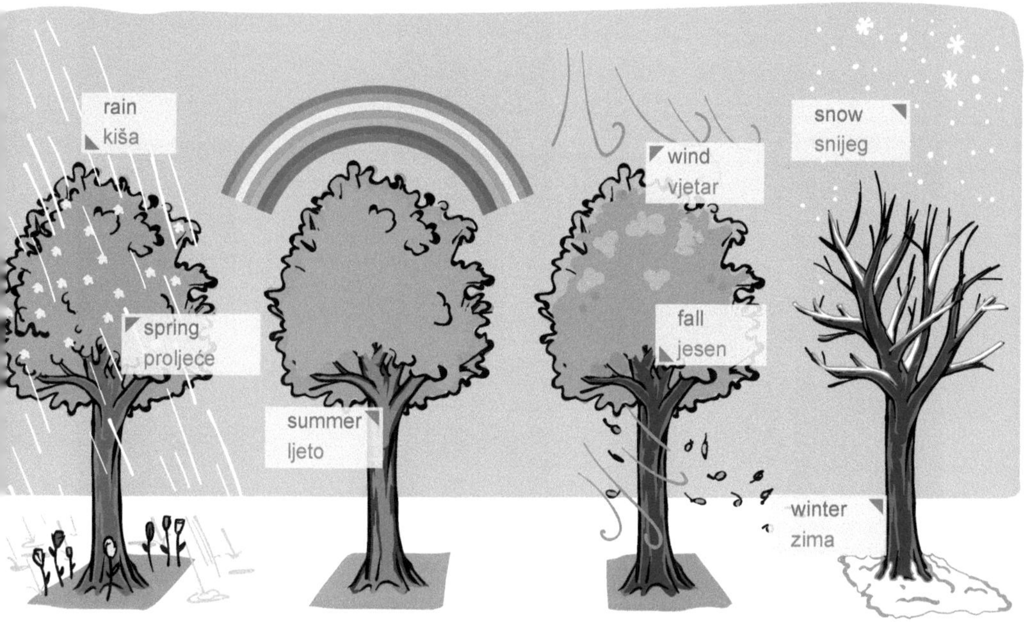

weather forecast

prognoza vremena

F C
120 40
90 30
60 20
30 10
0 0
-30 -10
-20

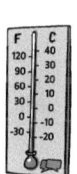

thermometer

termometar

sunshine

sunčev sjaj

cloud

oblak

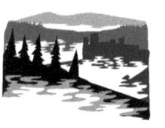

fog

magla

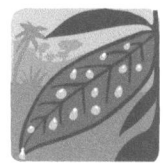

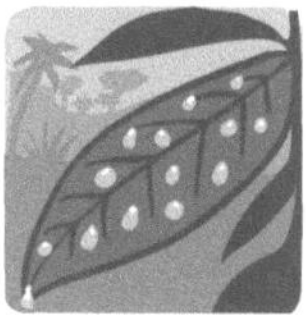

humidity

vlažnost vazduha

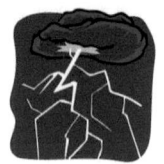

lightning
....
munja

thunder
....
grom

storm
....
oluja

hail
....
tuča, led

monsoon
....
monsun

flood
....
poplava

ice
....
led

January
....
januar

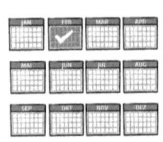

February
....
februar

March
....
mart

April
....
april

May
....
maj

June
....
juni

July
....
juli

August
....
avgust

year - godina

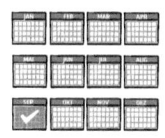

September
....
septembar

October
....
oktobar

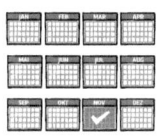

November
....
novembar

December
....
decembar

circle
....
krug

square
....
kvadrat

rectangle
....
pravougao

triangle
....
trougao

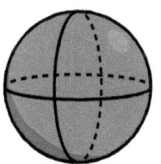

sphere
....
kugla

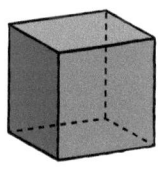

cube
....
kocka

white

bjel

yellow

žut

orange

narandžast

pink

pink

red

crven

purple

ljubičast

blue

plav

green

zelen

brown

smeđ

gray

siv

black

crn

a lot / a little
malo / mnogo

angry / calm
ljutit / miran

beautiful / ugly
lijep / ružan

beginning / end
početak / kraj

big / small
veliki / mali

bright / dark
svijetlo / tamno

brother / sister
brat / sestra

clean / dirty
čist / prljav

complete / incomplete
potpun / nepotpun

day / night
dan / noć

dead / alive
mrtav / živ

wide / narrow
široko / usko

edible / inedible

ukusno / neukusno

evil / kind

zao / prijatan

excited / bored

uzbuđen / dosadan

fat / thin

debeo / mršav

first / last

najprije / najkasnije

friend / enemy

prijatelj / neprijatelj

full / empty

pun / prazan

hard / soft

trvd / mekan

heavy / light

težak / lagan

hunger / thirst

glad / žeđ

ill / healthy

bolestan / zdrav

illegal / legal

ilegalan / legalan

intelligent / stupid

inteligentan / glup

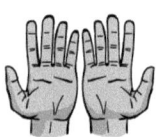

left / right

lijevo / desno

near / far

blizu / daleko

opposites - suprotnosti

new / used

nov / polovan

nothing / something

ništa / nešto

old / young

star / mlad

on / off

uključeno / isključeno

open / closed

otvoreno / zatvoreno

quiet / loud

tiho / glasno

rich / poor

bogat / siromašan

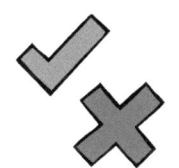

right / wrong

tačno / pogrešno

rough / smooth

hrapav / glatak

sad / happy

tužan / srećan

short / long

kratak / dug

slow / fast

spor / brz

wet / dry

mokro / suho

warm / cool

toplo / hladno

war / peace

rat / mir

0

zero

nula

1

one

jedan

2

two

dva

3

three

tri

4

four

četiri

5

five

pet

6

six

šest

7

seven

sedam

8

eight

osam

9

nine

devet

10

ten

deset

11

eleven

jedanaest

12

twelve

dvanaest

13

thirteen

trinaest

14

fourteen

četrnaest

15

fifteen

petnaest

16

sixteen

šesnaest

17

seventeen

sedamnaest

18

eighteen

osamnaest

19

nineteen

devetnaest

20

twenty

dvadeset

100

hundred

sto

1.000

thousand

hiljada

1.000.000

million

milion

languages
jezici

English
engleski

American English
američki engleski

Chinese Mandarin
kinesko mandarinski

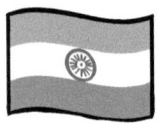

Hindi
hindi

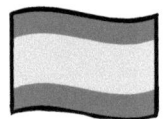

Spanish
španski

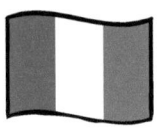

French
francuski

Arabic
arapski

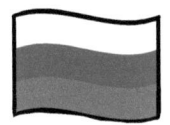

Russian
ruski

Portuguese
portugalski

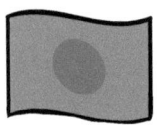

Bengali
bengalski

German
njemački

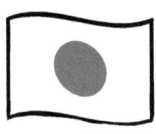

Japanese
japanski

I
ja

you
ti

he / she / it
on / ona / ono

we
mi

you
vi

they
oni

who?
ko?

what?
šta?

how?
kako?

where?
gdje?

when?
kada?

name
ime

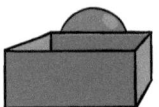

behind

iza

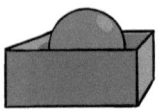

in

u

in front of

pred

over

iznad

on

na

under

ispod

beside

pored

between

između

place

mjesto